KOREAN FOLK SONGS
COLLECT

24 TRADITIONAL FOLK SONGS FOR INTERMEDIATE LEVEL PIANO SOLO

한국민요모음집

ARRANGED BY LAWRENCE LEE

ISBN 978-1-4234-9042-5

HAL•LEONARD®
CORPORATION

7777 W. BLUEMOUND RD. P.O. BOX 13819 MILWAUKEE, WI 53213

In Australia contact:
Hal Leonard Australia Pty. Ltd.
4 Lentara Court
Cheltenham, Victoria, 3192 Australia
Email: ausadmin@halleonard.com.au

Visit Hal Leonard Online at
www.halleonard.com

PREFACE

Korea is a country in far east Asia located between China and Japan. A nation of peace-loving people, Korea withstood countless invasions from many countries and preserved its singular national identity for over 4,000 years. Korean art is characterized by its use of space and uncontrived simplicity.

The 24 arrangements presented in this book represent Korea's storied cultural legacy. Many of them are still sung today. These songs are filled with sincere expressions of love, joy, hope, and hard work, but also sadness and struggle for survival.

I would like to extend my personal thanks to Ms. Jennifer Linn for the artistic and practical guidance for the project, Dr. Jeehai Song for the advice on piano writing, and also Ms. Jisun Lee for providing vital information on Korean folk music.

Explanation of Korean pronunciation:
a - as in "la"
eo - as in "fun"
o - as in "doe"
u - as in "noon"
eu - as in French "les"

ABOUT THE ARRANGER

Lawrence Lee is a versatile Korean American composer, songwriter, and jazz pianist. Growing up in both the United States and South Korea, Lee deeply absorbed the two distinct cultures, which have greatly influenced his music. He graduated with a BA degree in music from the University of California, Berkeley, where he studied composition with John Thow, Jorge Liderman, and Yiorgos Vassilandonakis; jazz piano with Mark Levine, Frank Martin, and Ken Berman; and conducting with David Milnes. He is currently pursuing a PhD in composition at the University of California, Los Angeles where he has been honored with the *Henry Mancini Award, Elaine Krown Klein Fine Arts Scholarship* as well as numerous other awards. In addition to writing music, Lee has performed as a pianist and singer, and has experience in film scoring, choral directing, live sound engineering, production and contemporary Christian worship music. His experience teaching piano and music theory privately for several years brings a unique blend of culture, composition, and pedagogy to the *Korean Folk Songs Collection*. www.LawrenceLee.com

TABLE OF CONTENTS

ENGLISH TITLE	KOREAN CHARACTERS	PRONUNCIATION

NOTES ON THE KOREAN FOLK SONGS

ARIRANG (page 8)

Arirang is a name for a metaphorical "pass" one has to climb over, symbolizing hardship. Although virtually every Korean can sing this song by heart, no one knows the exact origin or the meaning of the title. In the lyrics, the protagonist walks over Arirang pass longing for his or her departed lover. Because of its popularity through the country, many provinces have their own version of the song. However, this particular version, which is the most popular, is from Kyeonggi province.

HARVEST (page 10)

Harvest time is the merriest moment of the year in any agricultural society. Families and neighbors from all around Korea gathered to hold parties and sing this festive and graceful song to celebrate a successful year. *Pungnyeon* literally means "year of abundance."

THE GATE (page 11)

This is a children's game song that usually follows another game called "Catch the Tail." The children line up holding on to the waist of the person in the front of them. The leader calls by singing, "Gate keeper, gate keeper, please open the door!" Then the rest respond by exclaiming, "I have no key; I cannot open it!"

YEARNING (page 12)

Despite its seemingly optimistic tune, this song emerged out of hard times of the country. During Japanese occupation in the early twentieth century, people began to sing this song, longing for the king's return and with it, their independence.

FIVE HUNDRED YEARS (page 13)

In the past, many lower class Koreans perished from disease, famine, and war. This song from Gangweon province is filled with grief for lost love, family members, and friends. Mourning for the loved ones' departure, the singers wish longevity for their parents and themselves, desiring to live five hundred years.

CATCH THE TAIL (page 14)

Catch the Tail is another game song from Jeolla Province similar to *The Gate*. In this game, each team forms a line in which each person holds on tightly to the waist of the person in the front. The two teams mimic the way baby mice frantically follow their mother in a single line, making sure to go wherever their leaders choose. The goal of this game is for one of the players at the front of the two lines to catch the tail person of the opposing one and then exclaim, "I caught it!"

DANCE IN THE MOONLIGHT (page 16)

In olden times when the moon reached its biggest and brightest, women from southern Jeolla province would gather outside, form a circle hand-in-hand, and dance together until the morning. Just like the previous song, the dance begins slowly at first, and then gradually accelerates so that the dancers eventually need to leap around. It usually lasts all night long and thus the leader constantly has to create new lyrics to keep it going.

FUN IS HERE (page 18)

Everybody loves to have fun! Peasant neighbors from Gyeongsang province often gathered outdoors with many different instruments and sang this song out loud while joyfully dancing and wishing for *pungnyeon* (year of abundance). The song usually begins slowly, but then gradually speeds up as the fun grows.

YOU AND I (page 19)

This is an elegantly simple love song from Jeju (Cheju) province. Jeju-do is the largest island of Korea, located in the south, and has nurtured its own unique culture.

JINDO FIELD SONG (page 20)

Farmers from Jindo Island in Jeolla province sang this song while laboring in the field. It is more than a work song because it also contains a wealth of profound life messages on death, separation, and one's proactive acceptance of the sad reality.

AUTUMN IN THE CITY (page 21)

Modern Industrialization caused many people living in rural areas of the country to move to cities. There were opportunities and dreams, but there were also struggles and nostalgia. This beautiful song from Hamkyung province colorfully depicts a lonesome scene of a new city, in which autumn leaves fall and crickets chirp.

WILD HERBS (page 22)

This is a work song popular throughout the country. A singer, while collecting wild herbs, names different herbs and plants and describes them with interesting onomatopoeia and alliteration.

BOAT SONG (page 24)

Row your boat! *Guhmoondoh* was a large island in Jeolla province, inhabited mostly by fishermen. To expedite their travel, sailors would paddle together in rhythm creating an energetic groove in which to sing their song.

LULLABY (page 26)

This simple song, with its soothing and gently rocking melody, is a lullaby mothers still sing for their children to this day.

THE PALACE (page 27)

Gyeongbokgung is the palace in Seoul where the kings resided. It was once destroyed during a war, but then was rebuilt in order to restore the central authority. This song is believed to have been sung by workmen as they labored. It is pompous, bold, and optimistic.

FLOWERS (page 28)

Flowers is a romantic song that portrays a young girl clumsily digging up the roots of bellflowers while dreaming about the love of her life.

THE MILL (page 29)

There once lived a penniless master *Geomoongo* (zither) player. Trying to comfort his starving wife, he began to play a sound resembling a grinding mill pounding on rice, and thus created an illusion of a mountain of food. Lured by the strikingly similar sound, his neighbors gathered together to listen to his music.

CRICKET (page 30)

Sareum means cicada in the Hwanghae dialect. In the evening, the somber, dull whine of the cicadas brings a sense of nostalgia to all those who hear them.

THREE-WAY JUNCTION (page 32)

This jolly and carefree song from Chungcheong province is about a well-known three-way junction in Cheon-An. Travelers from the southern and southeastern area must pass this junction in order to reach Seoul, the capital.

CHESTNUT (page 34)

Chestnut is another cheerful and lighthearted song from Gyeonggi province that is often sung as a game song. Each singer takes a turn in a call-and-response fashion, and the melody and lyrics change constantly from one singer to another.

THE PIER (page 36)

Near cape *Jangsan* in Hwanghae province is a pier called *Monggeumpo*, which is known as a summer resort because of its white sand and green pine trees. *The Pier* depicts a dazzling view of the cape and pier, painting a picture of the daily lives of native fishermen who live nearby.

BIRDIE, BIRDIE (page 38)

During the busy harvest season, children would follow their parents to the fields and sing this song to the birds. This seemingly naive song is a tribute to a legendary war hero.

WATERFALL (page 40)

Deep in Mount Cheon-ma, in Gyeonggi province, is a magnificent waterfall, *Bakyeonpokpo*. This song celebrates love that is deeper than this waterfall.

HAN RIVER (page 42)

The Han river is the major river in Korea, flowing from *Taebaek* mountains through Seoul to the West Sea. People from different social standings sang this song on a leisurely boat ride while enjoying the delightful scenery of Han riverside.

ARIRANG
아리랑

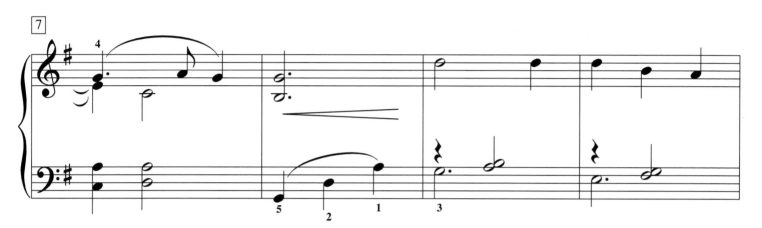

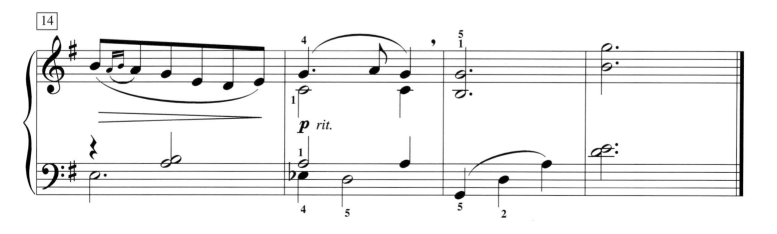

HARVEST
풍년가

Jubilant ($\quad$ = 120)

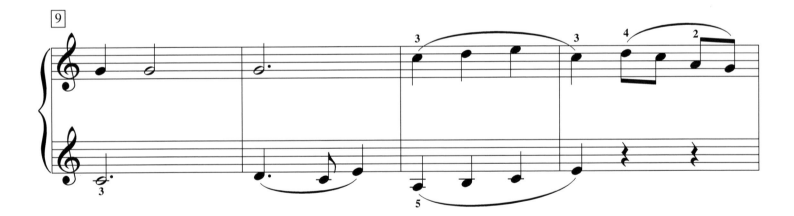

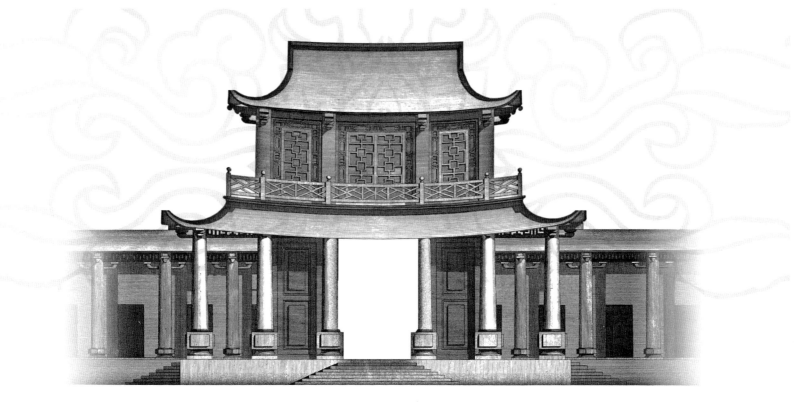

THE GATE
대문놀이

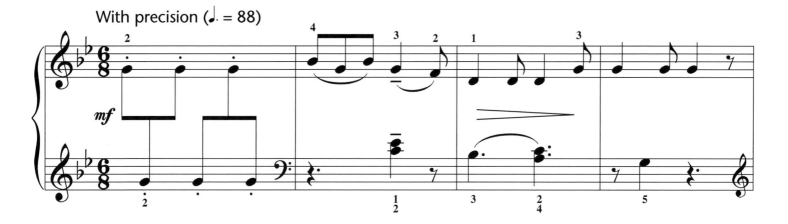

With precision (♩. = 88)

YEARNING
닐리리야

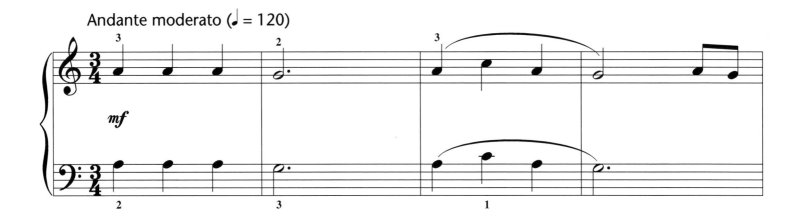

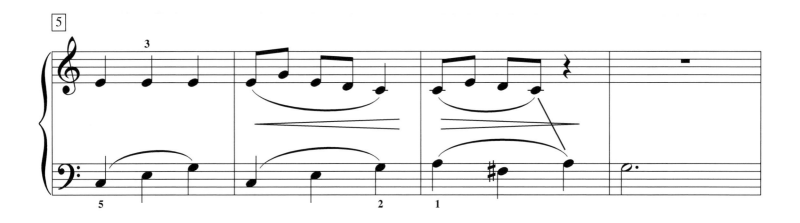

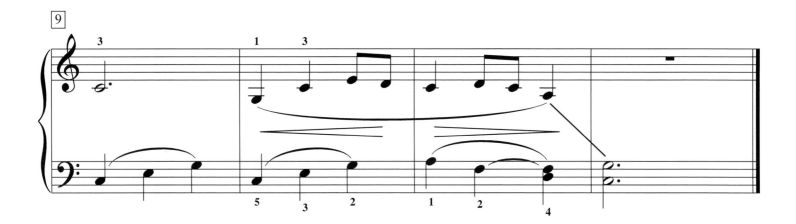

FIVE HUNDRED YEARS
한오백년

Andante (♩ = 88)

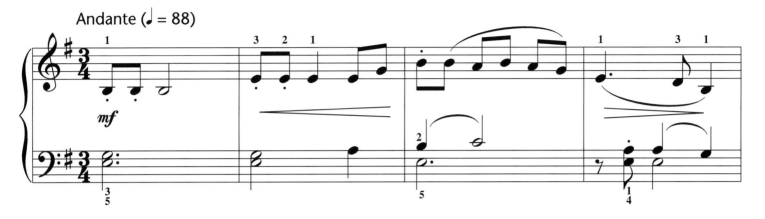

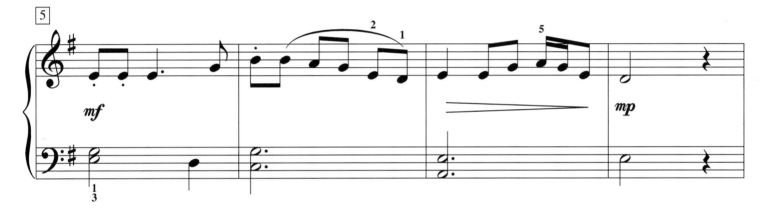

CATCH THE TAIL
쥔쥐새끼

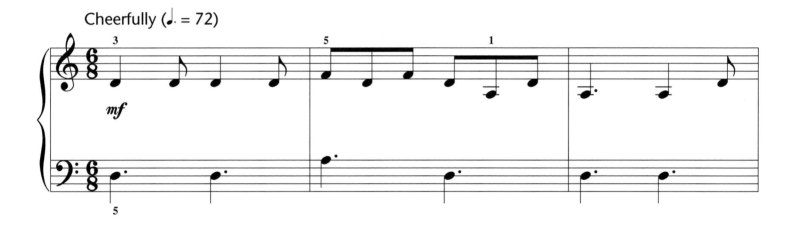

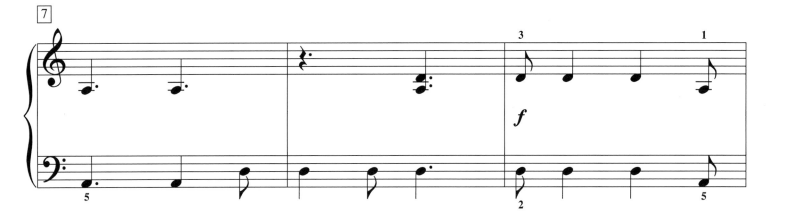

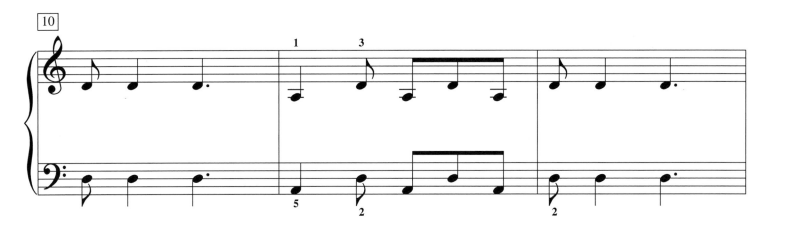

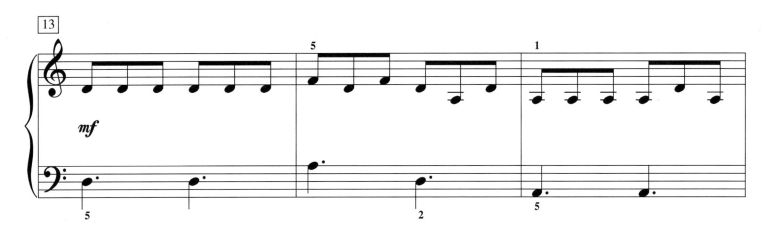

DANCE IN THE MOONLIGHT
강강수월래

Flowing (♩ = 152)

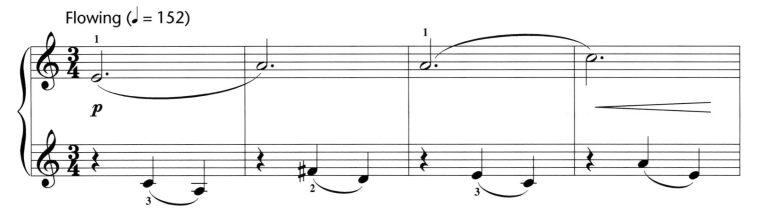

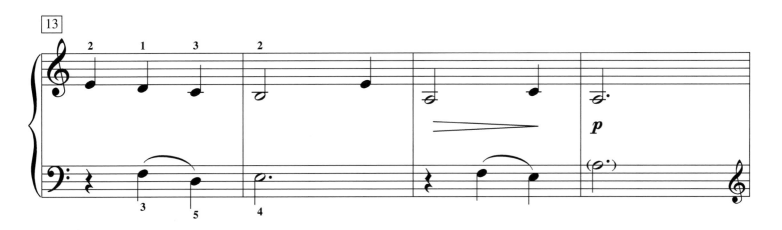

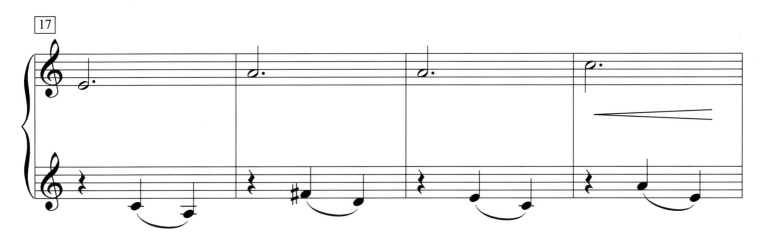

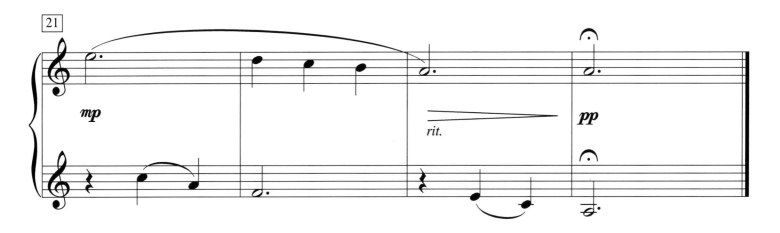

FUN IS HERE
쾌지나 칭칭나네

Bouncy (♩. = 84)

YOU AND I
너영 나영

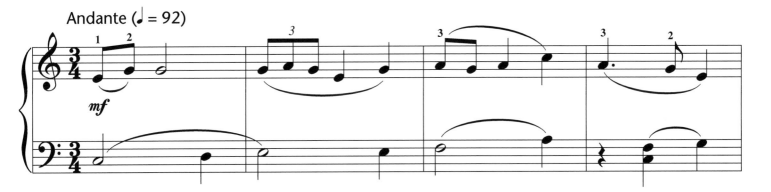

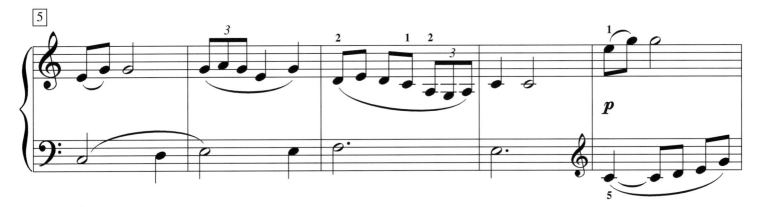

JINDO FIELD SONG
진도들노래

Tranquillo (♩ = 112)

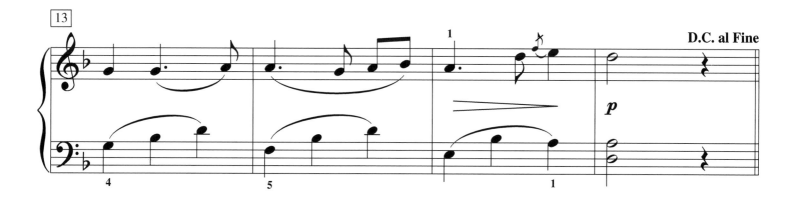

AUTUMN IN THE CITY
신고산타령

Solemnly but deliberately (♩. = 60)

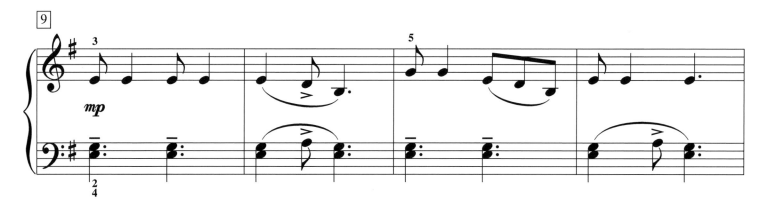

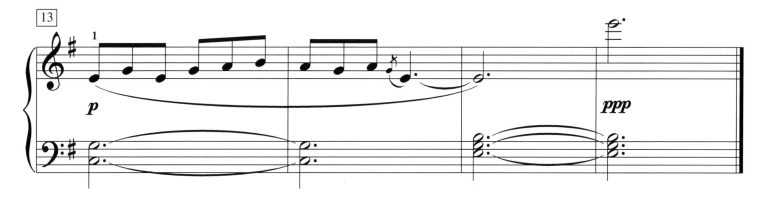

WILD HERBS
나물노래

Tenderly (♩ = 104)

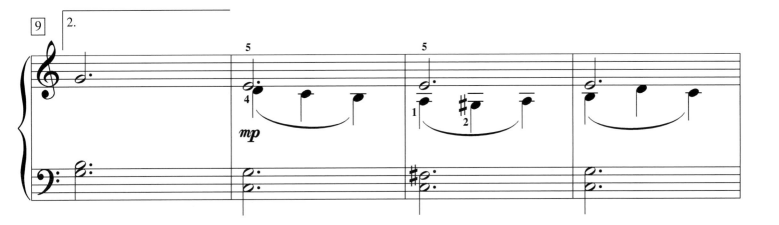

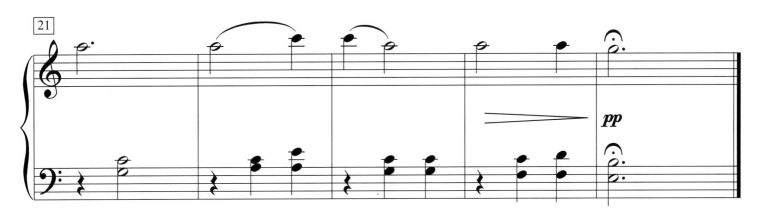

BOAT SONG
거문도 뱃노래

Energico (♩. = 100)

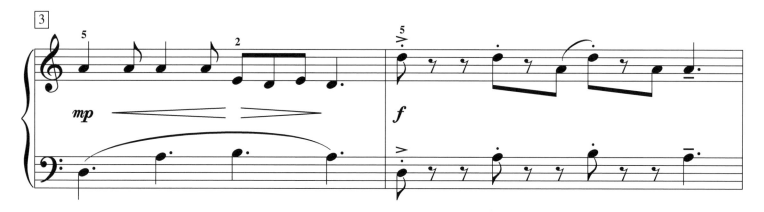

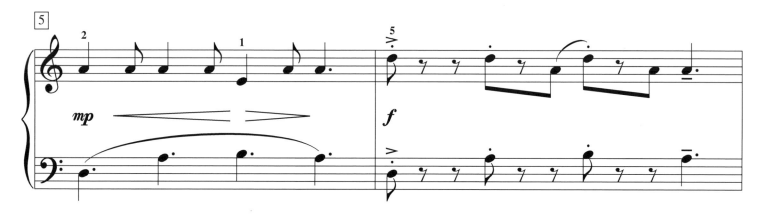

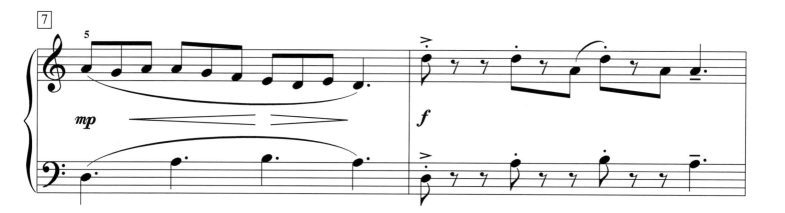

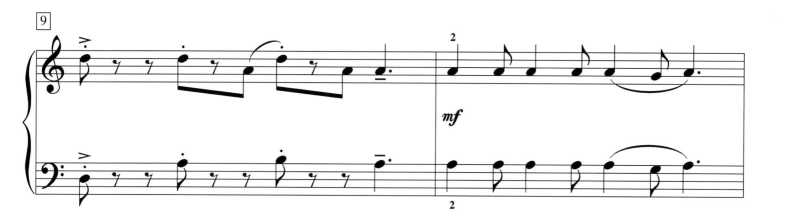

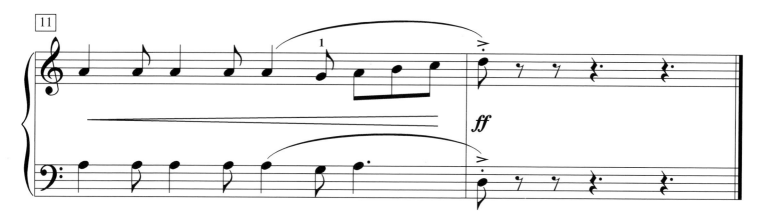

LULLABY
자장가

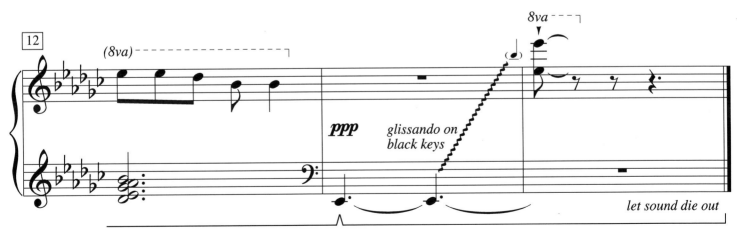

THE PALACE
경복궁타령

Grandioso (♩ = 80)

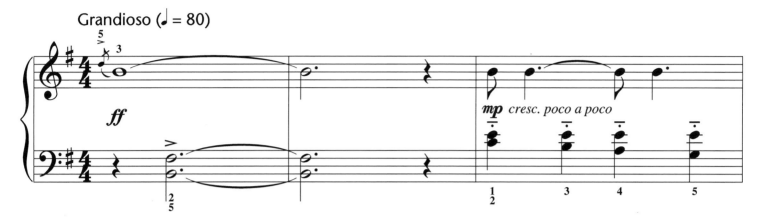

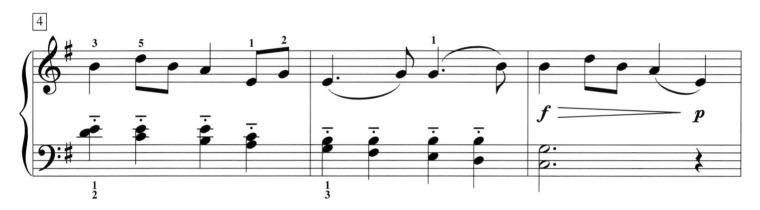

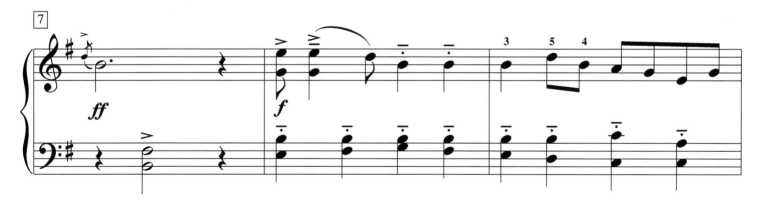

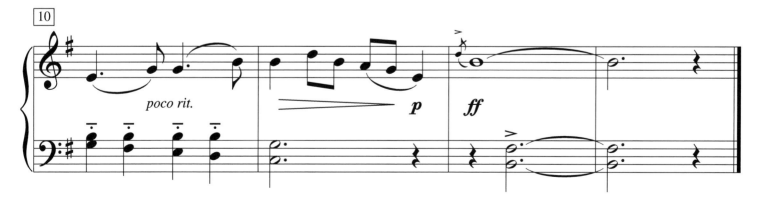

FLOWERS
도라지타령

Andantino affettuoso (♩ = 124)

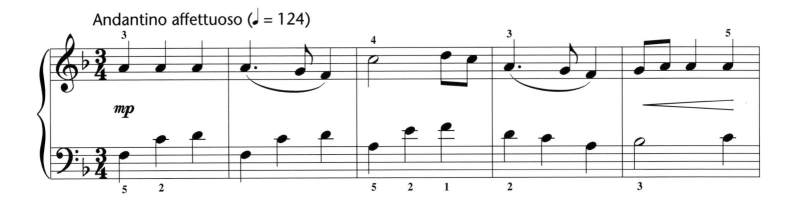

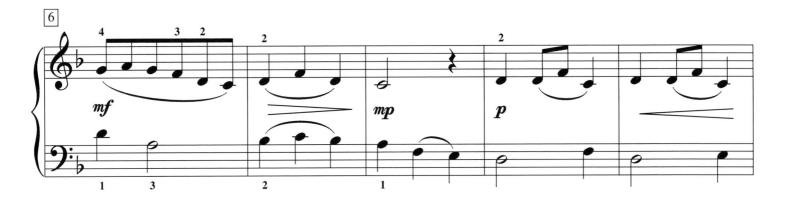

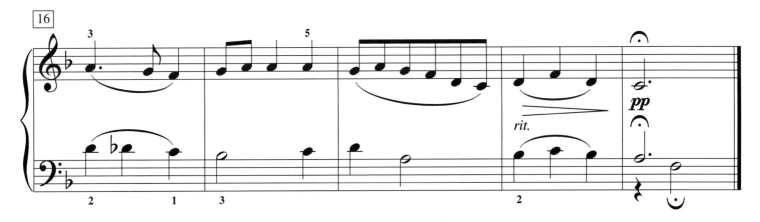

THE MILL
방아타령

Walking with groove (♩. = 80)

gently tap the
wooden part
of the piano

CRICKET
싸름

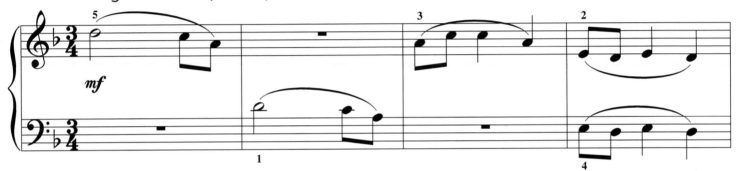

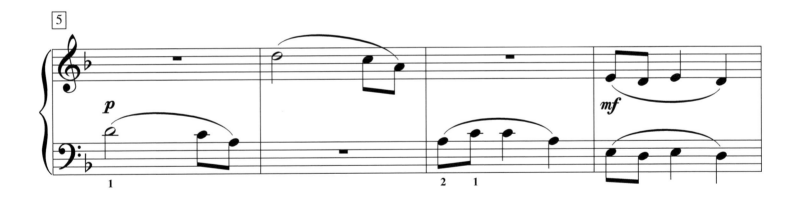

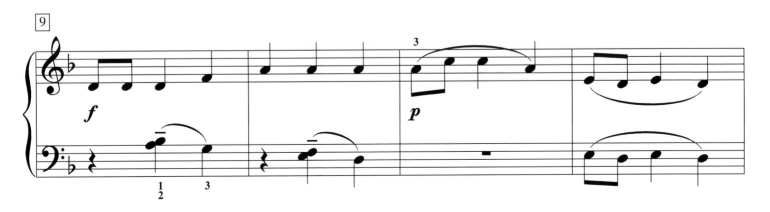

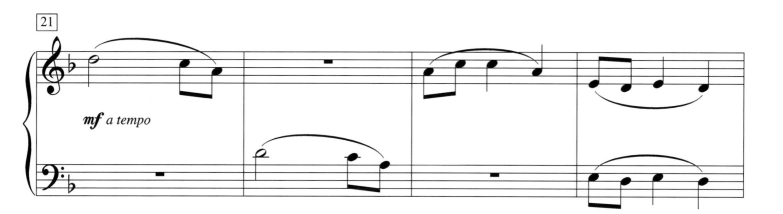

THREE-WAY JUNCTION
천안 삼거리

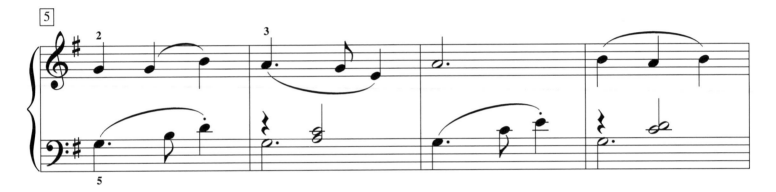

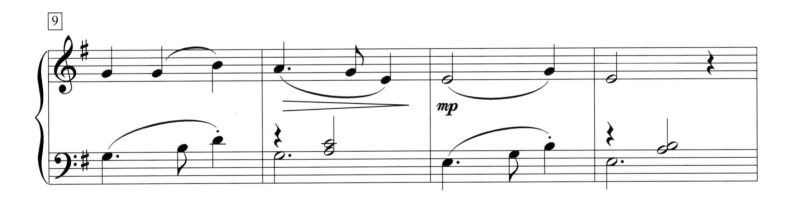

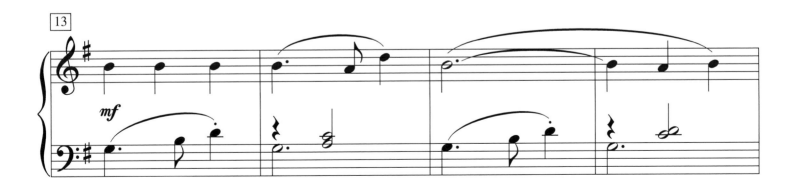

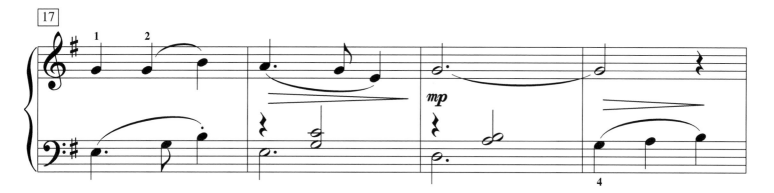

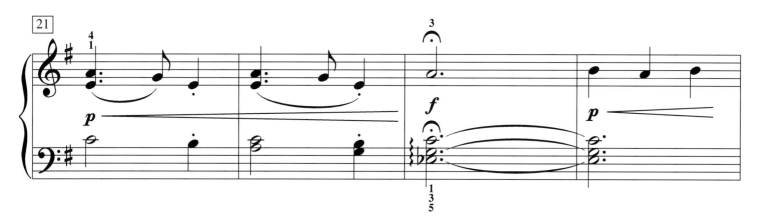

CHESTNUT
군밤타령

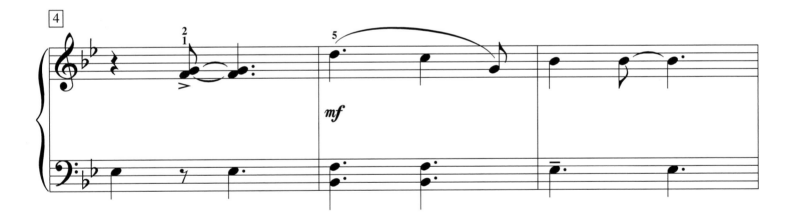

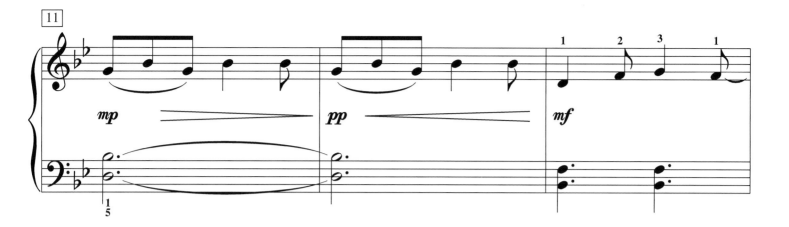

THE PIER
몽금포타령

Andantino cantabile (♩ = 124)

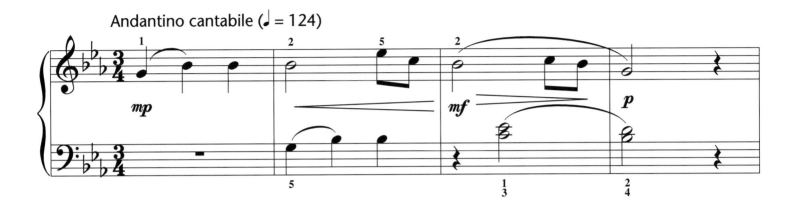

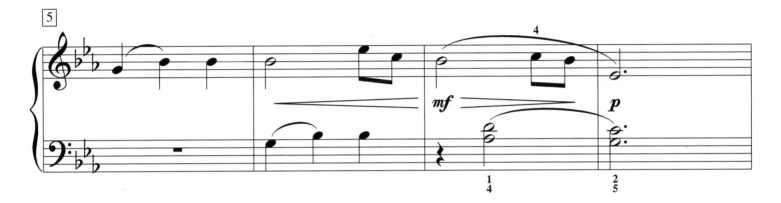

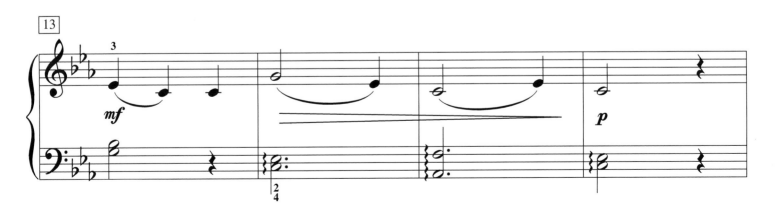

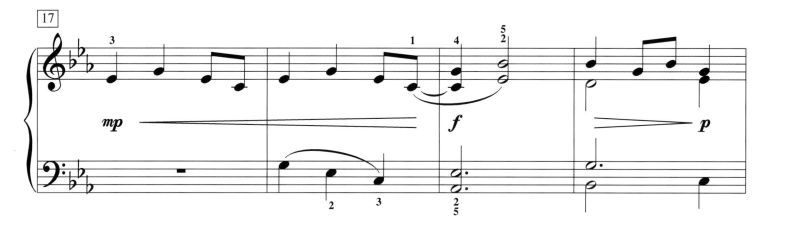

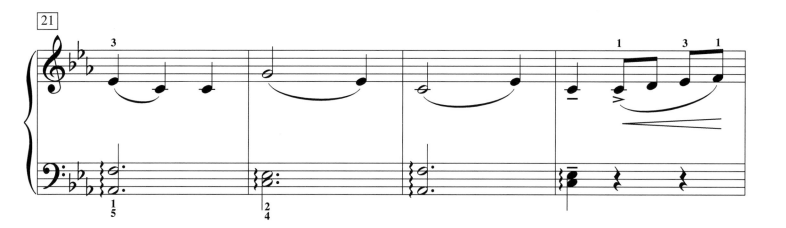

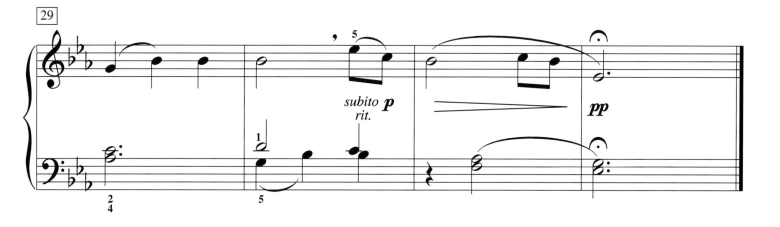

BIRDIE, BIRDIE
새야 새야

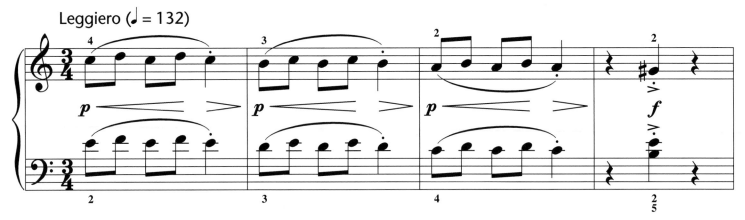

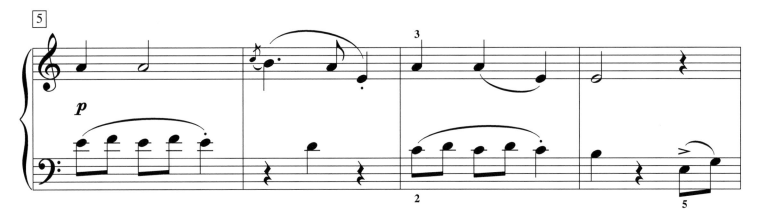

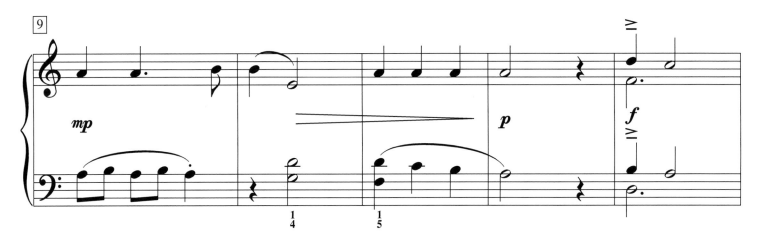

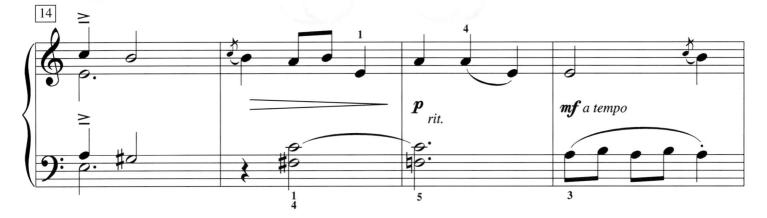

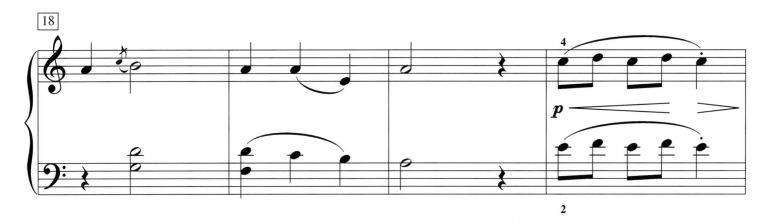

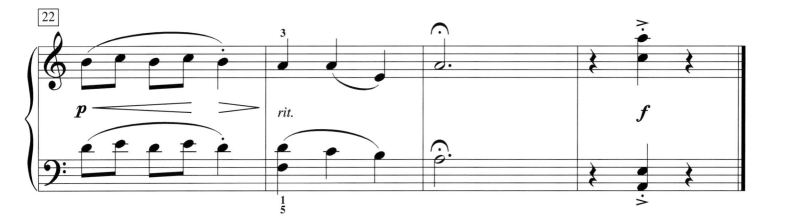

WATERFALL
박연폭포

Moderato nobilmente (♩ = 116)

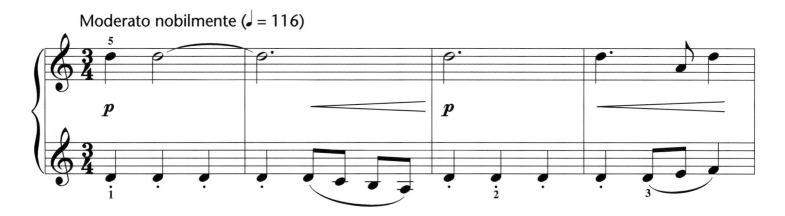

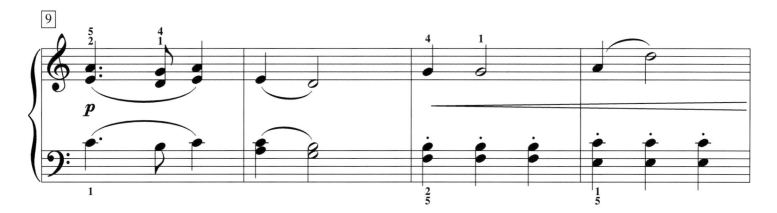

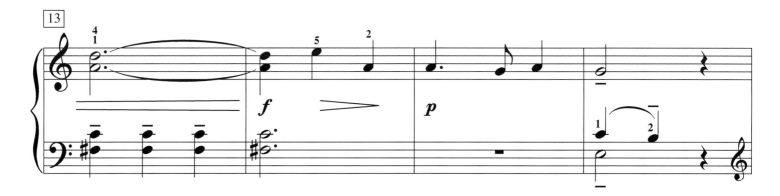

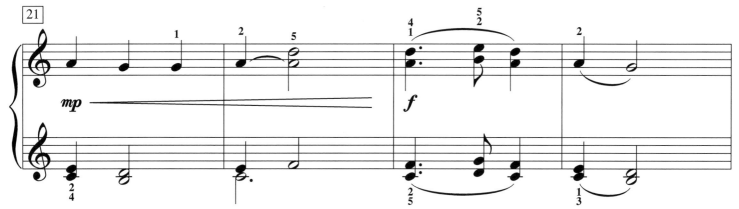

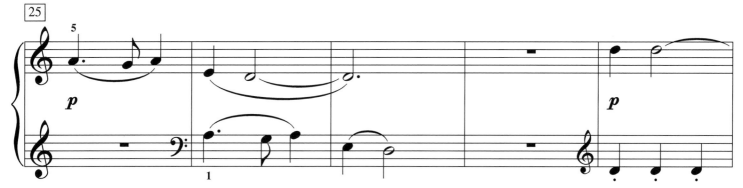

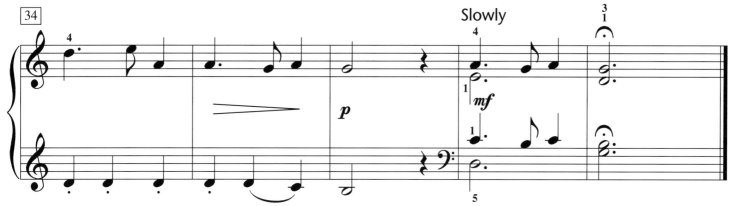

HAN RIVER
한강수타령

Tempo rubato (♩. = c. 48)

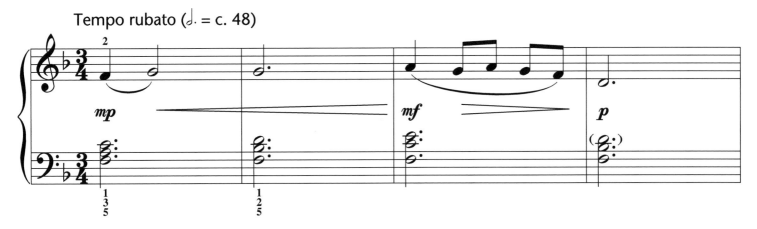

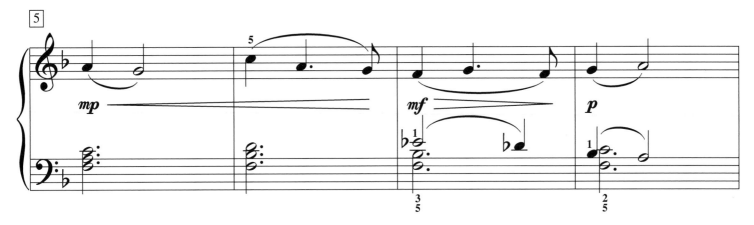

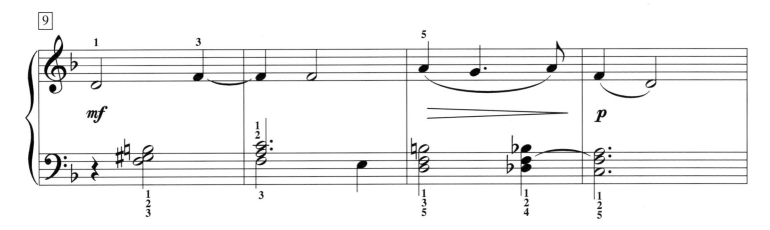

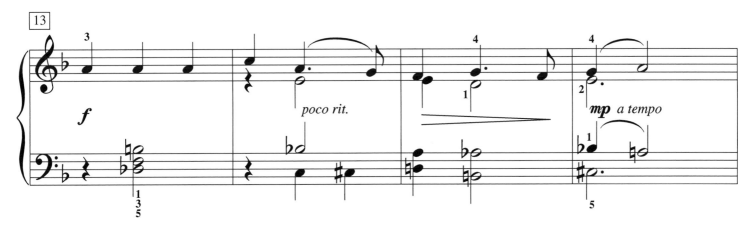

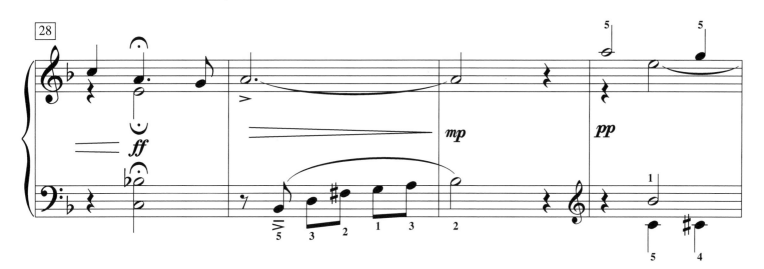

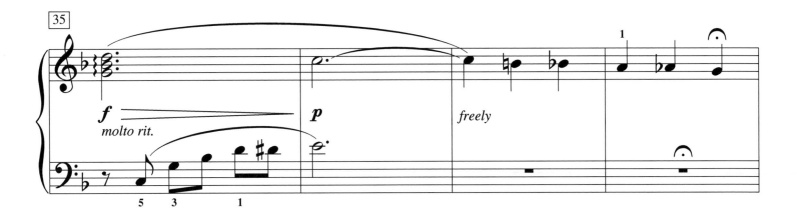

Tempo Primo

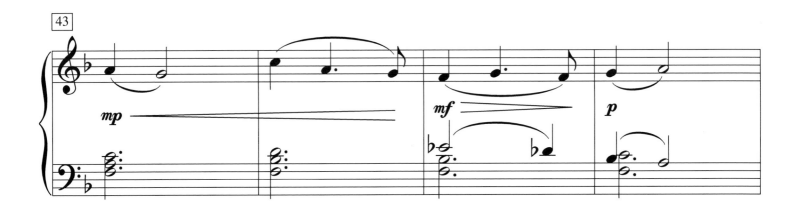

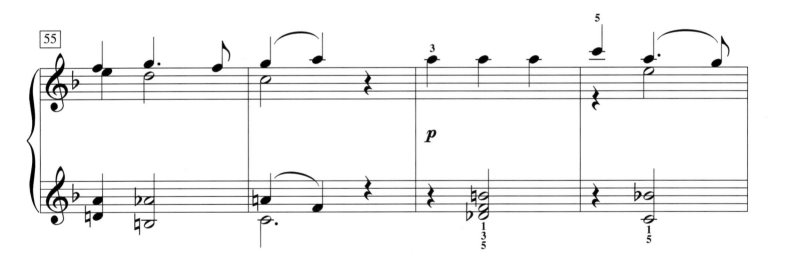

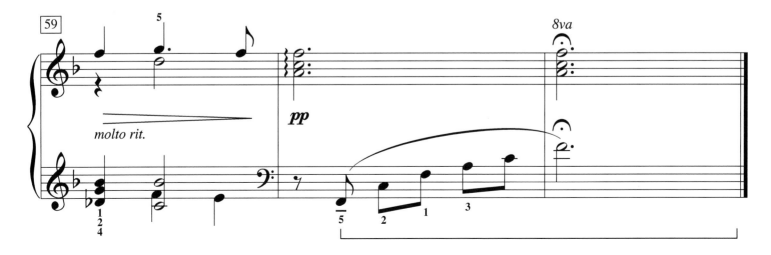

MAP OF KOREA

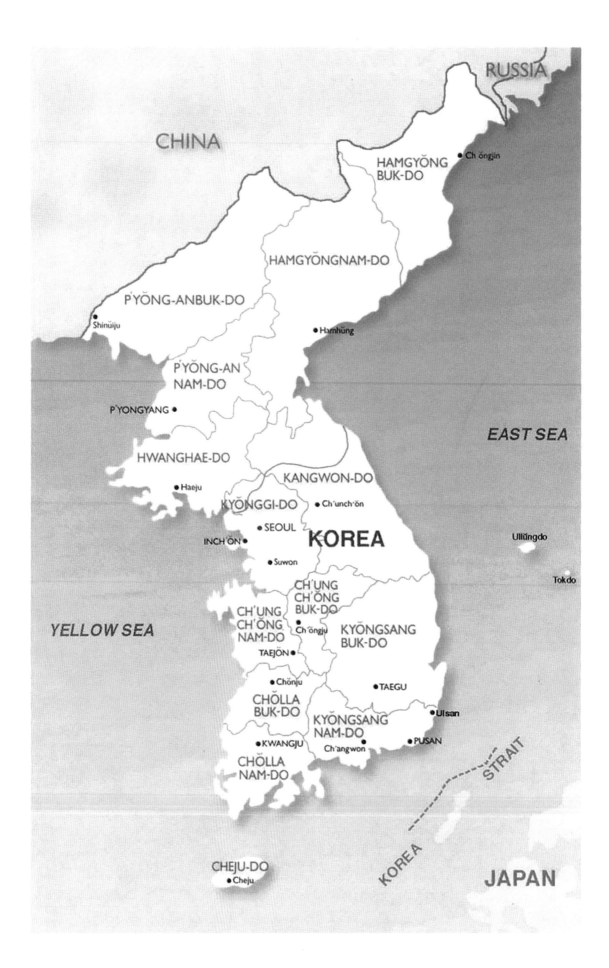

FOLK SONG COLLECTIONS
FOR PIANO SOLO

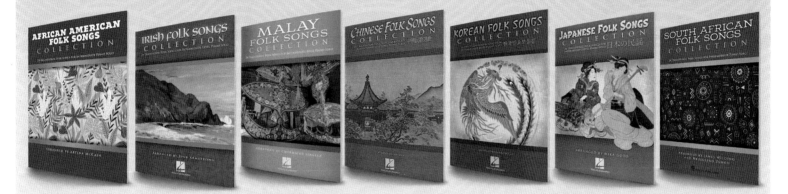

Introduce piano students to the music of world cultures with folk songs arranged for intermediate piano solo. Each collection features 24 folk songs and includes detailed notes about the folk songs, beautiful illustrations, as well as a map of the regions.

AFRICAN AMERICAN
arr. Artina McCain

The Bamboula • By and By • Deep River • Didn't My Lord Deliver Daniel? • Don't You Let Nobody Turn You Around • Every Time I Feel the Spirit • Give Me That Old Time Religion • Guide My Feet • I Want Jesus to Walk With Me • I Was Way Down A-Yonder • I'm a Soldier, Let Me Ride • In Bright Mansions Above • Lift Ev'ry Voice and Sing • Little David, Play on Your Harp • My Lord, What a Morning • Ride On, King Jesus • Run Mary Run • Sometimes I Feel Like a Motherless Child • Song of Conquest • Take Nabandji • Wade in the Water • Warriors' Song • Watch and Pray • What a Beautiful City.
00358084 Piano Solo...$12.99

IRISH
arr. June Armstrong

As I Walked Out One Morning • Ballinderry • Blind Mary • Bunclody • Carrickfergus • The Castle of Dromore (The October Winds) • The Cliffs of Doneen • The Coolin • Courtin' in the Kitchen • Down Among the Ditches O • Down by the Salley Gardens • The Fairy Woman of Lough Leane • Follow Me Up to Carlow • The Gartan Mother's Lullaby • Huish the Cat • I'll Tell My Ma • Kitty of Coleraine • The Londonderry Air • My Lagan Love • My Love Is an Arbutus • Rocky Road to Dublin • Slieve Gallion Braes • Squire Parsons • That Night in Bethlehem.
00234359 Piano Solo...$12.99

MALAY
(MALAYSIAN AND INDONESIAN)
arr. Charmaine Siagian

At Dawn • Chan Mali Chan • C'mon, Mama! • The Cockatoo • The Curvy Water Spinach Stalk • Five Little Chicks • God Bless the Sultan • The Goodbye Song • Great Indonesia • It's All Good Here • The Jumping Frog • Longing • Mak Inang • Milk Coffee • The Moon Kite • Morning Tide • My Country • Onward Singapore • Ponyfish • Song for the Ladybugs • The Stork Song • Suriram • Trek Tek Tek • Voyage of the Sampan.
00288420 Piano Solo...$10.99

CHINESE
arr. Joseph Johnson

Beating the Wild Hog • Blue Flower • Carrying Song • Crescent Moon • Darkening Sky • Digging for Potatoes • Girl's Lament • Great Wall • Hand Drum Song • Homesick • Jasmine Flower Song • Little Cowherd • Love Song of the Prarie • Memorial • Mountaintop View • Northwest Rains • Running Horse Mountain • Sad, Rainy Day • Song of the Clown • The Sun Came Up Happy • Wa-Ha-Ha • Wedding Veil • White Flower • Woven Basket.
00296764 Piano Solo...$12.99

KOREAN
arr. Lawrence Lee

Arirang • Autumn in the City • Birdie, Birdie • Boat Song • Catch the Tail • Chestnut • Cricket • Dance in the Moonlight • Five Hundred Years • Flowers • Fun Is Here • The Gate • Han River • Harvest • Jindo Field Song • Lullaby • The Mill • The Palace • The Pier • Three-Way Junction • Waterfall • Wild Herbs • Yearning • You and I.
00296810 Piano Solo...$12.99

JAPANESE
arr. Mika Goto

Blooming Flowers • Come Here, Fireflies • Counting Game • The Fisherman's Song • Going to the Shrine • Harvest Song • Itsuki Lullaby • Joyful Doll Festival • Kimigayo • Let's Sing • My Hometown • Picking Tea Leaves • The Rabbit on the Moon • Rain • Rain Showers • Rock-Paper-Scissors • Sakura • Seven Baby Crows • Takeda Lullaby • Time to Go Home • Village Festival • Where Are You From? • Wish I Could Go • You're It!
00296891 Piano Solo...$12.99

SOUTH AFRICAN
arr. James Wilding, Nkululeko Zungu

The Axe Cuts the Thorn Tree • The Clouds They Thunder •The Crowing of the Rooster • The Doves Above • God Bless Africa • Here Comes the Alibama • I Have a Sweetheart in Durban • Jan Pierewiet • Mama, Who Is This? • Our Dearest Mothers • Sarie Marais • Sugar Bush • They Say There's a Man in the Moon • What Have We Done? • and more!
00368666 Piano Solo $12.99

HAL•LEONARD®

halleonard.com

*Prices, contents and availability
subject to change without notice.*

POPULAR SONGS

HAL LEONARD STUDENT PIANO LIBRARY

The **Hal Leonard Student Piano Library** has great songs, and you will find all your favorites here: Disney classics, Broadway and movie favorites, and today's top hits. These graded collections are skillfully and imaginatively arranged for students and pianists at every level, from elementary solos with teacher accompaniments to sophisticated piano solos for the advancing pianist.

Adele
arr. Mona Rejino
Correlates with HLSPL Level 5
00159590.............................$12.99

The Beatles
arr. Eugénie Rocherolle
Correlates with HLSPL Level 5
00296649............................. $12.99

Irving Berlin Piano Duos
arr. Don Heitler and Jim Lyke
Correlates with HLSPL Level 5
00296838.............................$14.99

Broadway Favorites
arr. Phillip Keveren
Correlates with HLSPL Level 4
00279192.............................$12.99

Chart Hits
arr. Mona Rejino
Correlates with HLSPL Level 5
00296710.............................$8.99

Christmas at the Piano
arr. Lynda Lybeck-Robinson
Correlates with HLSPL Level 4
00298194.............................$12.99

Christmas Cheer
arr. Phillip Keveren
Correlates with HLSPL Level 4
00296616.............................$8.99

Classic Christmas Favorites
arr. Jennifer & Mike Watts
Correlates with HLSPL Level 5
00129582.............................$9.99

Christmas Time Is Here
arr. Eugénie Rocherolle
Correlates with HLSPL Level 5
00296614.............................$8.99

Classic Joplin Rags
arr. Fred Kern
Correlates with HLSPL Level 5
00296743.............................$9.99

Classical Pop – Lady Gaga Fugue & Other Pop Hits
arr. Giovanni Dettori
Correlates with HLSPL Level 5
00296921.............................$12.99

Contemporary Movie Hits
arr. by Carol Klose, Jennifer Linn and Wendy Stevens
Correlates with HLSPL Level 5
00296780.............................$8.99

Contemporary Pop Hits
arr. Wendy Stevens
Correlates with HLSPL Level 3
00296836.............................$8.99

Cool Pop
arr. Mona Rejino
Correlates with HLSPL Level 5
00360103.............................$12.99

Country Favorites
arr. Mona Rejino
Correlates with HLSPL Level 5
00296861.............................$9.99

Disney Favorites
arr. Phillip Keveren
Correlates with HLSPL Levels 3/4
00296647.............................$10.99

Disney Film Favorites
arr. Mona Rejino
Correlates with HLSPL Level 5
00296809 ....$10.99

Disney Piano Duets
arr. Jennifer & Mike Watts
Correlates with HLSPL Level 5
00113759.............................$13.99

Double Agent! Piano Duets
arr. Jeremy Siskind
Correlates with HLSPL Level 5
00121595.............................$12.99

Easy Christmas Duets
arr. Mona Rejino & Phillip Keveren
Correlates with HLSPL Levels 3/4
00237139.............................$9.99

Easy Disney Duets
arr. Jennifer and Mike Watts
Correlates with HLSPL Level 4
00243727.............................$12.99

Four Hands on Broadway
arr. Fred Kern
Correlates with HLSPL Level 5
00146177.............................$12.99

Frozen Piano Duets
arr. Mona Rejino
Correlates with HLSPL Levels 3/4
00144294.............................$12.99

Hip-Hop for Piano Solo
arr. Logan Evan Thomas
Correlates with HLSPL Level 5
00360950.............................$12.99

Jazz Hits for Piano Duet
arr. Jeremy Siskind
Correlates with HLSPL Level 5
00143248.............................$12.99

Elton John
arr. Carol Klose
Correlates with HLSPL Level 5
00296721.............................$10.99

Joplin Ragtime Duets
arr. Fred Kern
Correlates with HLSPL Level 5
00296771.............................$8.99

Movie Blockbusters
arr. Mona Rejino
Correlates with HLSPL Level 5
00232850.............................$10.99

The Nutcracker Suite
arr. Lynda Lybeck-Robinson
Correlates with HLSPL Levels 3/4
00147906.............................$8.99

Pop Hits for Piano Duet
arr. Jeremy Siskind
Correlates with HLSPL Level 5
00224734.............................$12.99

Sing to the King
arr. Phillip Keveren
Correlates with HLSPL Level 5
00296808.............................$8.99

Smash Hits
arr. Mona Rejino
Correlates with HLSPL Level 5
00284841.............................$10.99

Spooky Halloween Tunes
arr. Fred Kern
Correlates with HLSPL Levels 3/4
00121550.............................$9.99

Today's Hits
arr. Mona Rejino
Correlates with HLSPL Level 5
00296646.............................$9.99

Top Hits
arr. Jennifer and Mike Watts
Correlates with HLSPL Level 5
00296894.............................$10.99

Top Piano Ballads
arr. Jennifer Watts
Correlates with HLSPL Level 5
00197926.............................$10.99

Video Game Hits
arr. Mona Rejino
Correlates with HLSPL Level 4
00300310.............................$12.99

You Raise Me Up
arr. Deborah Brady
Correlates with HLSPL Level 2/3
00296576.............................$7.95

HAL•LEONARD®

7777 W. BLUEMOUND RD. P.O. BOX 13819 MILWAUKEE, WI 53213

Prices, contents and availability subject to change without notice. Prices may vary outside the U.S.

Visit our website at **www.halleonard.com**